T0156694

East

OF

Goodbye

East
OF
Goodbye

POEMS

RICHARD CLAUDE VALDEZ

EAST OF GOODBYE
POEMS

iUniverse books may be ordered through booksellers or by contacting:

iUniverse
1663 Liberty Drive
Bloomington, IN 47403
www.iuniverse.com
1-800-Authors (1-800-288-4677)

ISBN: 978-1-4917-9051-9 (sc)
ISBN: 978-1-4917-9050-2 (e)

Library of Congress Control Number: 2016903797

Print information available on the last page.

iUniverse rev. date: 04/25/2016

To my dear son **Ricardo Claude**

ACKNOWLEDGEMENTS

To Troy for his indispensable computer skills and patience

Photo by Bernard Valdez

East of Goodbye is essentially a *vade mecum* of goodbyes—adieu, farewell, separation, severance and death; all reflected through nature and the human heart. The author struggles with the heart's expression of youthful passion and that of the age of compassion.

Throughout this volume the author battles with this equipoise; and this struggle finds much substance in the expressions of youthful optimism and that of aged resignation.

In the poem, **This and More is but the Love so Shared and Given**, he proposes that joy and sorrow is but, "to assume this stigmata", borne of the conditions of both passion and compassion-- in struggle for the silence of the sacred heart.

In the last poem of this volume, **All Done**--with self-resignation to a quest unrequited-- he surrenders; "Sweet running tears all mopped up, memories drowned in a bottomless cup".

East of Goodbye may be viewed perhaps as the last volume in the trilogy—the conclusion with
Aperture as the genesis and **Promise of the Rainbow through My Tears** as the nucleus.

TABLE OF CONTENTS

ALPHABETICAL
TABLE OF CONTENTS

This and More is but the Love so Shared and Given

This and more is but the love so shared and given.
Some will never know how grand the silken braid is woven.
To assume this stigmata--
Sharing both joy and sorrow,
Embracing the bitter thrust of time's own decaying law,
And there to wither with the petals of a flower.

To exchange passion for compassion,
To barter in the market place of hearts and tenderness
Is but to be a moneylender--
Counting up the profit in a slice of gain.

To this end; lost in timbre of warm temperament
We stumble at the thought--
Blind with the sharpness of the truth it bears.

With choice instead to fold them both--
Passion with compassion,
Under the apothecary's mix,
Upon the potter's wheel of care and mould,
To hold,
Steady in the blood red silken lace--
To trace,
A dance so bold;
And there to fashion a new star
On points of light both near and far,
That can be seen through night and day
A brilliance that lights the way.

To find comfort though,
In its never-ending reach,
Joining all who dare to water at this trough.
Take heart; we all who suffer in the sigh of passion,
And melt in the heat of osculation,
And languor in mute embraces,
And die in a giving so great and complete
That want and need is lulled
And put to bed with rounded stomach.

It is not lost.
There is no end.
No death! To such a wholesome gift--
"Rejoice!"
"Give thanks and praise"
For we have sung a song that has no end,
A melody that finds within its throb
A golden knob
That turns the dark to Light.

Such gift is ours to treasure and to hold
This heavenly psalm;
"Kneel in homage!"
"You, unworthy and untold"
Who dare not taste this sacred balm.

In Response

Now we speak in riddles.
Now we speak in murky mysteries.

Imagine, after epochs of experience
We speak in veiled shadowy innuendos;
Perhaps the result of time—
That cruel side of days
When the heavy weight of unforgiving circumstance
Drags an iron chain across the tender paths we cut;
That tender side of a turning sky
Once a- bleed with starry gleams of unrepentant giving.

But cantillate instead with melodies--
The orisons of communal souls;
Stain with sighs and music a dancing heart,
And press upon its virgin canvas an effulgent scene
Of rolling limbs-- as the sea rolls,
Giving up a rolitant cry
And welcoming embrace upon a yawning shore.

Let us paint in place of riddles,
Our names with rhythmic brushes of scenic contentment:
"To whisper!"
"Intone!"
"To chant!"
"And sing with amain!"
Proclaim with mighty sweetness
The choreography of a new dance—
A yet unwritten symphony rearranging heaven's song forever.

Passion for Compassion?

Still the Neanderthal—
Crawling along the belly of emotion,
Drinking up passion,
Turning up the spine at times to scope beyond the hilltops
For unsuspecting prey;
Yet, straining in the barter of "passion for compassion"—
A trade that does not auger well
Nor find a fruitful market.

Perhaps locked in his lair,
Layered in the dark of night will come an angel
To touch his savagery,
Turning his appetites from touch and taste
To a crying heart seeking Communion.

Until such time, the digit claw of taste and touch
Still seeks a prey full recompense
To coil and wretch in the breach of passion;
And then to sleep in sleepless vision of mutual contentment,
Having crossed over once again
Into the arms of a savage sea.

To Stand Empty

Empty now to stand empty--
Hollow as a drum;
Discarded and all used up.
A hollow well,
Save the shell,
Left by to echo
Deep and hollow
In unmelodious staccato.

The cruise is dry
The must all gone
The wine all drained.

The bees all flown,
Abandoned nests
Hollow rests
Where dripped the gold
That stung a waiting tongue with honeyed sweetness.

The stump remains.
Remains of Evergreen, Oak and Willow,
Hugging the fields dead and fallow,
Long lost, long dead life's youthful callow.

In Remorse

We cannot bear to harvest such tenderness so ripe and raw--
Sentient even to a gentle thought,
This fruit we once nurtured.

To pluck from another's vine--
Yield fashioned by caring hands to a comforting trellis,
Is but to taste the first tear of childhood.

It could have been grand;
It would have been so fine,
But flies this deed
On its journey into a world we cannot enter.

The cord now severed,
The chord now in discord so long, so long ago;
That neither soul can find—even in earnest quest—
Frayed ends with which to neither join nor bind nor tether.

Everyman his one true love,
Every man his great epiphany,
Everyman his sorry blunder,
Every man his close kinship,
--There breathes no man without his tragedy.

Love, epiphany, blunder, kinship, tragedy—
Such makes us whole;
We shoulder them upon our journeys—
Wherever we rest,
Whenever we kneel;
They are the stripe and scar of whip and scourge
That burns with brine of sweat well purged.

Perhaps, when that final cloud becomes a tear
That drowns us in a pool of thought--
Drawing this filmy curtain to a close;
We will with genuflection aver upon a weighty bosom,
Velleity's meagre cry-- osculation pure,
The wound we opened with the scythe of our own forging;
And in humble sigh lay down the burden of this voyage;
To plenary prayer we grant unction!

Legerity's Longing

"If this be earth!"
"O God!" What then must Eden's worth
Bestow In riches for the soul,
Her beauty to extol
Upon us all.
There loom the gates that we have all been keys
To enter in; and hook our hearts upon the starry seas.
"Come home you weary soldier"
"Come taste what you have sought"
"With pain and blood and fear all bought"
"Shed the chains of iron now rusted with your tears,
"Come! Taste the fruit of Peace your heart now bears".

To Time

O Time!
Illusive spell who runs away with our youth.
O Time, with unrelenting sooth
You leave your footprints on our faces,
Scoured out traces--
Lines of weathered sentience;
And in our eyes a reflected scene
Of where our hearts and souls have been;
And so we pass.
Alas; decked out in tomorrow's suit,
For soon, our ephemeral salute
To hang our hats high up on heaven's rung--
Our songs all sung
--Having passed this way for the last time--
We, a band of Angels,
We, on wings sublime.

I Hear You Calling

Your call today settles my heart into a gentle throb,
Remembering your calls so long ago
When we were young in love and loved in youth--
Our dance tireless and naked under the light of heaven.

And that sigh; holding its form upon your lips
Never to wither on your redolent breath.
Tireless sweet thoughts, warm memories-- never restful
Except to light upon your soft warm bosom.

Your call today finds much remembrance:
Tenderness so tender that even a butterfly would crush--
That a petal would bruise
That a leaf would shatter
That a blossom would smother
That a kiss would sear.

Your call today set the ocean on its guided path
And the moon to find comfort in its orb.

Your call today lulls the restless ocean to a restful sleep
And the curve of heaven's bowl smoothes itself upon the mountain
tops-
Genuflection in praise to the cradle of the valley;

I hear your call.
I answer!
-Willingly crossing over.

Poezie to the Tulips of Keukenhof

O! To be like tulips
Planted in God's Garden,
Each one a row of silken lips
With many colours laden.

Each Tulip different in its own,
Each colour bright and true,
By the Master's hands all grown--
Some white some red some blue.

If only we could be like tulips,
Bright souls of light and harmony,
We could touch with fingertips,
Heaven in its glory.

If only we would learn from them
And all our warring cease--
Then we could reach the leaf and stem
To taste the fruit of peace.

To My Brothers

Walk with me by the water
Clasp my hand at the shore
Let our hearts beat together
And our love yearn for more

Let us always remember
Those boyhood pranks galore
And nights of peaceful slumber
And days with laughter soar

"Now rest near the rolling river"
"And watch the cascade pour"
Let our paths ne'er, ne'er sever--
Bound by fraternal lore.

To Surrender!

Know now that all must have its time.
To allow much to pass away unencumbered by the chains of memory
Is but wisdom's code.
The pleasant too must give way to a shape void of the sting of feeling,
And left to die its death,
As it lives its life:
Free to dance;
To linger
Free,
To wallow;
Its own rhythm, its own heart beat
Stilled by its own will.

Alas, but still to hold for the last time
Something so treasured,
That to release would bring the skies to earth.
But to have not the courage nor the will to fill
A rub that invites the balm of Angels;
Instead to wait for the crumble and the run,
The crack and the break
All fissured in and wide;
Is not to be!
--For such a love that makes the heavens gasp.

With resignation's due—
To you, sweet you
In reverence true;
I surrender to memory.

Saying Goodbye to Their Father

Alone
To grieve,
To see them leave.
His eyes clouding over with the mist of pain;
Perhaps to never lay his eyes upon his sons again.
His sons; borne from his manhood now stilled by age,
This old quiet pensive sage
Now hugging sorrow--
His only comforting pillow.

Memories of his boys running into the wind,
That very wind--many years later--that lit their sails,
Never more to see his lighthouse again.

And so to slip away
In the early light of day,
In his silent ship he let slip
The anchor, fixed and deep,
Watching for the last time
The final sunset seep
Over the lip of life;
And then to rest
In the burning west,
To weep.
And now to sleep.

In the Windstorm

In the windstorm wild and wailing
Amidst a coal-black obsidian night
Watching from heaven's balcony this Crucifixion:

Tree and limb and crown of branch straining in might of weight and
twist and turn
Of fierce and cruel wind;
Piercing through with spear and sickle and scythe--
The summer-scorch and sap succumbs.

At Morning's Light all laid out
The rout about of limb and leaf and trunk and break of branch—
Broken bones and blood of limbs and stumps sneered and grinning raw--
Confusion in a dead heap pile.

Save one!
Triumphant!
Serene!
The Tree of Life.
The Evergreen.

To Sleep on Many a Strange Kindness

To sleep on many a stranger's kindness;
Many a cradle swaddled up in dreams serenaded by a sympathetic moon,
Whose moonbeams run like tears
Shed for this bent-over traveller.

Under an obsidian sky,
Moving in a cloud of darkness,
Steadying a crouching corner a lost traveller kneels.

This dismembered heart; lost, lame and cast off;
Knee deep in heart's desire to grasp the uncertainty of tomorrow's dawn;
To hold the defenceless hope of youthful dreams
That drinks deep in solitude.

Such task is ours; without question or consequence,
To lay a gentle pillow under this head of worry.
To father this willing orphaned heart
Is but to hug the fragile infant in comforting lullaby.

Photograph of a Lost Time

Under the eerie mist of time,
Our souls dissolve;
Leaving memories scarred upon an ancient landscape
Torn away by years.

We reflect; we remember; we dream-
Perhaps of reliving a pristine tenderness,
A virgin tide that washed the smiles of our ancestors:
Long ago,
Long gone,
Long swallowed up,
Long lost,
Long forgotten,
Except in our longings.

Idle Moon

And what say the moon?
Does it hum a Berceuse?
Does it dream of a time long ago when lovers were true lovers
And love as lovers do?
Or does it stand sadly by in a face of golden light
Shedding its own tears; bright
Fingers searching out the dreams of lovers past;
Remembering and reminiscing when the spell was cast
Upon an unsuspecting heart.

Will you beckon it to sleep, rousing its indolent gaze?
Perhaps to awaken a vagabond heart
Searching out its dream in another land
Beyond this world,
Such that love can only savour when this earthly light is no more.

O so sad a moon!
Unemployed in the sky
When so many hearts lay idly by.

Moth

Amidst the triangular blue spruce,
Encircled by the sacred arms of nature's embrace,
Butterflies stir--
Sitting upon my grateful shoulders,
Fanning with their scented wings
A heart filled with wonderment.

A reverent wind enters in to kiss a cheek.
Two solitary leaves shake hands in a free-fall from across the pathway.
To all this harmonious bliss,
Add the singing stream,
Keeping rhythm with the heart of this gentle song.

But, under the thick dark growth
The Gypsy moth gives birth.
She turns in a dance,
Pushing forth her young,
Bellowing in silence,
Drowning in her sightless blood.

O hated intruder-Lymantria!
Desperate and lost upon an ancient land.
Set free and abandoned you turn
Voracious and unrepentant—
-A grudgeful restitution-
For slavery's chains;
Gluttonous retribution for an orphan's plight.

Behold! A Miracle smiles under the Maple leaf:
A gift of the wind;
Cradled in comfort,
Swaddled in silence;
Her life giving young.
Her sacrifice made,
She turns on her wings,
And in graceful salute gives up her sentence.

Sitting between the blue spruce to think of God,
Watching this sacrifice played out before my eyes:
This caterpillar in infant form,
Sleeping in comfort,
Waiting for its Angel's wings to blossom.

"Fly soon soft spirit!"
"Beneath the towering spruce"
"Home to the nest above the clouds".

Summer's Fall

Today shapes the bones of a fall day;
So soon in this season of a bare summer green—
Green trees remember;
"Too soon", they murmur under their breath of leaves;
Green tongues humming a hymn of hopeful green eternities,
Eternising dendrochronology's circular dance to the seasons.

This day wipes away the sweat of a laughing summer;
And teases the full flaired fruitfulness with the hint of a premature shawl—
Save the wildness of frivolous colour
Dipped in the damp, dropped sweetness of a righteous rain.

Today fashions a coming which does not wear a winsome welcome.
The imposter sneaks in under the covers of rain.
This phantom falling equinox reminding us
That harvest ingathering unexpectedly falls upon an undiscerning heart;
And Goodbyes are forever.

Jerusa

And where is she?
Amerigo's feminine mate-
Christened by Waldeemuller's Chrism-
The Florentine's vagabond son;
That land protector and harbour of innocents:
Impotent!
Guilt ridden!
Useless.
A modern Rome in ashes;

And it its throne of majesty
The planted prince of plunderers complacent rests;
Harping the chorus of Machiavellian rhymes--
Malcontent and discontent—
Suspicion's deceptive web.
Corinthian's; "God of Peace in disorder,"
Nailed in sacrifice to history's legacy when injustice ruled with chains.

Standing pale and anemic, the city on the hill-
White and worn; kneels in suppliant's defeat,
While the Chalice runneth over with the blood of the beguiled.

Leaves

Leaves fall and are dissolved away by time.
The ever welcoming earth feeding off her offspring.
Sad to see them blown away by the ever persistent wind,
Blind to its faithful chore,
Unseen and unrewarded for its diligence.
At times, when I sit alone in the green silent park
Under the blue spruce that cradles my thoughts,
I think of leaves--falling and ever falling;
Being replaced as waves
In that large and yawning basin the sea.

I sometimes hear my name-- a whisper upon a falling leaf
Or branch or shy and gentle twig,
Choosing precisely the spot where it must rest
Tenderly I pray,
Upon a soft and welcoming earth:
And there to rest
In quiet sleep;
And then to sing
With joyful din-
Peacefully amongst its welcoming kin.

East of Goodbye

Woman! Woman!
Your name usurped by your charms,
Unshackled and unbridled by my call,
Free and wild as wind above the trees,
Salted fresh and dipped amongst the waves
In the girth and breath and taste and bouquet of an intruding sun.

Woman! I call, but you do not answer;
My eyes, tethered to your image,
I watch you walk away and my heart follows you home;
And turn with weary heart to a sky that leaves no trace of your passing.

Woman, buried you are in the peat of my heart--
Curled in the soft milky pith of tenderness;
You sing like the wind in the tree tops
A song only to me; a *Liebestod!*
And I weep in unison.

"Woman, eponymous to love-
Hear a supplicant's orison!"
Resigned in heart to victory pyrrhic,
Still, I eat your vision, blood and bone
And lay you bare-
Licking up the stains of tears--
Left over embers of an embattled heart.

In vain velleity's loss
Still; I burrow like a worm
And lay my scent within your form.
But alas!
Too ephemeral you are;
Your Evanescence star
An Alpenglow;
Dripping down the legs of memory.

Goats and Monkeys

Which sword first sliced the salted waters of my island-home?
--Those of goats or those of monkeys?

One wears horns the other paws
One garrottes the other claws.

All wrapped up in the tongue of falsehood
They both carry the loud silence of the tomb.
Listen to the bleat and chatter of fools-
Self proclaimed prophets whose salvation
Perverts the sacredness of forgiveness,
To the sword of retribution.

Goats and monkeys
Horns and tails
One bellows the other rails.

The village fools made king and queen,
While the just and wise stand where they had been:
Impotent eunuchs
With tails of ducks
Wagging aimlessly their useless feathers
Soiled and stained by the mess of others.

Goats and Monkeys
Pigs and Donkeys.

Rooftops

Sombre shades of Autumn drapes its shadowy arms
  Across the shoulders of a resigning evening;
Rooftops still and brown crouch
  Within the shade of deepening shadows,
My heart hums a brown note;
  Preparing for the symphony of falling leaves,
As memories of a winsome summer
  Make way for the sweet sadness that is to come-
A Summer lost somewhere in thoughtless preoccupation
  And useless trails of journeys that meant nought,
Leaving emptiness wrought by wayward thought.

One solitary swallow sails past my window,
  Lost in the shuffle of a million feathers-
With wide eyed wildness seeking out the sunlight
  That calls like a haunting hunter's horn,
Stirring the shadows always shadows;
  Calling down the hounds of change
To pin down screaming and wailing
  The last rays of a Summer's day.
Over the rooftops the bold night walks;
  Washing away the tops of chimneys:
Closing windows,
Sitting boldly on my scene,
Stifling my sight to a premature surrendering:
  Of a night I do not welcome,
  Of stillness I do not embrace,
  Of darkening rooftops shadowy creep;
Yet, deep within the cell of mystery I weep-
As Archons dig and cover deep--
Rooftops melting into that moss of sleep.

Vignette

True love comes to we who wait
If we allow the hands of fate
To sift and weigh and guide the rate
That hearts in love must kiss and mate.

If patience be the wisdom's bait
And time be the courtly date
Then why to fret with anxious prate
"Have faith my sweet! It's not too late".

Talmid

The humble Talmid remembers well from whence he came.
He steady holds the oars;
Within its memory lays the truth to his journeys;
And why he languors upon a hostile shore.

Espied along the rolling seas loom
Shipwrecks--
Sails in droop, torn and tattered,
Ragged and raw from the winds held in arrogant fullness;
New lands discovered,
New dreams dreamt,
Only to be reminded that they had all been dreamt before.

From a distance calls the sounds foreboding—
Wailings left behind upon the rocks of refuge;
"Are you Eve?" he calls.
"I am Eimi!" the response.
Homer's eyes and Jason's might succumb.

Talmid both, they find "Sweet Water "there,
To drink deep from the four pillars of Eden,
The Heart from which Pison flowed—
Sweet Light that has no end,
Sweet Truth that cannot be profaned;
The Love Agape that defies dimension-
Chaste and undefiled
Vestal and virtuous without blemish
—unstained by the cunning hips of *Ego*.
The humble Talmid remembers well the path--
His journey home.

In Praise of Tears

What is this tear?
From whence its flow?
Not from the eyes I know.
It drains but from a tender sore-
An ancient and familiar door
That salts our souls as the sea salts the faithful shore.

"But what does it mean?"
This tear!

To watch an infant shed its tears is but to hold a beating heart--
To feel its pulse,
To hear its throb-
A weeping in its rhythm,
That eternal anthem in praise of life,
Calling us all to commonality;
That harmonious and recognisable family
Fused in mutual kiss of contentment.

Is then this tear the heart's sweet singing
Its liquid symphony?
A rivulet of sacrificial giving,
Liquid light from an open wound, flowing
Down the cross; redeeming.
This tear, is it then Salvation?

Joining all rivers of emotion-
One mighty wave flowing into one universal ocean;
In common transference exchanging light for Light.
This tear; this stream of sacred salt,
This graceful roll of quiet thunder,
Lumping all together that which is sacred in us,
This tear--this path of light;
This River Pison in which we dip our oars,
Where she first wept her tears;
And stained his cheek with Sphinxian mystery

So graceful, so magnificent this tear;
We hear its rolitant fall from Eden's skies;
To see it rain, to catch its beams upon a grateful hand--
Such Baptismal and Matrimonial joining of our hearts with His.
This tear that lights our path to the gift of unction.

Our journey lit, we sail home upon its starry Light,
Riding the crested waves of tears of light of praise;
This tear that points the way to covenant with rainbow and with
blood--
This Baptismal font from which our fears are washed away--
This Eucharistic Wine.

To Her

Too much!
It is too much;
Too weighty a prize,
Too terrible a pain.
Nails through the bone,
A heart alone
Under the dark night's sky
Beating down a rhythmic cry
To unmerciful tenderness.

To stand alone and afraid,
To have lost the bare brittle
And tempered steel of will and mettle;
To stand now, naked in the icy wind and sing your praises,
Is but to bleat like a shorn sheep,
Running over the cliffs to the open jaws of sea worn rocks
To break my bones.

All this add the *malde mer* of empirical loss;
This twist and turn and torque of inflamed sorrow-
A siphonal suctioning of the heart's marrow.

Bare and broken,
Rent and riven,
Devoid of courage;
I dare not Love this way again!

There is a Great Loss Here

There is a great loss here,
Perhaps unaware
The eagle flies alone over the tops of mountains,
Leaving its mate behind to settle the score of unity's prize--
Aloneness.
That shriek that tears the night-sky,
Calling back memory's
Gentleness.
That peat and pith within the womb's--
Oneness.
In silence its wings dip behind the mountains arch,
Falling away
In feathered farewell to Goodbye's endlessness.

Saying Goodbye at the River Thames

When the freshly salted tears of a sad parting
Dries upon the cheek of friendship,
Perhaps we may muster heart's courage
To trace the sentient sweetness of a time so well spent;
And dip into those moments scented with goodness.
But, until then, we savour the ripeness of memory,
And allow the days to simmer deep;
Deep down in our garden of thoughtful reminiscences.

We said Goodbye with boyhood tears
And our eyes—though wordless—
Drew back the covers of a lifetime,
To reveal what we had always known—
A friendship that is timeless.

We may perhaps—if time be merciful—
Venture out again into a world that we can share and savour
As friend and brother.

Until then—if the weather be kind—
And our sails are still full and set to the fair winds;
We can once more dip our ageing oars into the Thames;
Those sacred waters in which we wept-
Tears of a timeless friendship.

Paschal

Nailed to a tree.
Bound to the shroud of premature ash.
Praying for the sky to set it free.
Writhing in a cruel dance.
A sacrificial *Totentanz.*

In tribute to its imminent demise
Under the dark cross hunched over in prayer,
Giving off an incensed breath,
Standing upright in defiance of its mortality.

And I watch this ritual,
A lone gypsy bound and gagged;
Its wanderings entombed,
Counting out the flickers in its own time—
Flamed seconds in its drum roll.

Paschal in a lover's dance
Sensual and warm
In bright faerie trance,
Licking the air
Moving in a circle
Churning with a flare
A diminutive ell
Hypnotic in its spell.

Covered in white nakedness,
Pierced by a teasing taper
Raging silently;
Caught in a waxen tomb.

Singing for a finished time--
A threnody,
Quiet,
Regal as the Nazarene.
Rolitant and serene.

And in the rescue of a merciful dawn—
After the night has feasted on its flickering soul-
There, wrapped in a shrouded cloak of white,
Tears like larvae dripping down in funeral rite-
Stands a sacrificial tree chaparral;
Kneeling at its redemptive *Chapelle*-
The Eternal Paschal.

Calling Out

Streets are quiet
Winds are silent
Sky is asleep
Moon slumbers
Stars doze in the firmament
Phoebus hides in the vault of heaven.

Within this peaceful reservoir of repose and restfulness-
A heart wails,
Woeful and wanting.

A mighty gong echoes across the edge of time and space;
Calling, calling;
Calling out for those who seek his Grace;
For the hem of the raiment,
To wipe away their fears and tears.

Pigeon

Feathered butterfly sailing pass
The window glass;
Beauty in flight
Graceful and slight,
A swirl
A dip
A tight and tidy hip
Intent and precise in purpose.
An anxious freeze in flight,
With wing-full flair
Scratching out a plot of air
To lay its tense and tender toes upright
Upon the rails and rows
Of balconies;
Wide eyed and terrified
Looking down and side to side.

Yet, amidst this tranquil ballet upon the airy stage and sky
Some scene unsettles the soft sweet feathered Dove
In its course as it wings by;

For under the weather beaten *eve*
Hidden beneath the moss and scum
Of scale and slime--
Lines of snakelike trails run down to earth;
And there! Surreptitiously tempting--
Deceptively winking,
Stalks the cunning hellish hawk,
Waiting for its soul.

The Morning Broke

The morning breaks like the slow quiet dribble of a new born infant
--A drop at a time—
Down the fledgling chin of a new born day;
And the fresh spewing sunlight stretches its arms along the sleeping
floor,
Shooing away the last dregs of a lazy night.
Yawning, the dawn rolls over and slowly stands erect,
Kissing the window's glass with Incendiary embrace--
A wall of firelight burning up the last embers of a bleak and swarthy
night.

Why add to this miracle?
This mystery of manifestation,
This splendid uninterrupted syzygy of nature,
My least and lesser tatterdemalion presence
Upon a new creation;
But with grand accouchement,
Instead--with reverential genuflection
I withdraw;
Becoming a respectful voyeur to this wonder,
This sacred apothecarial mix of faithful travail,
This suckling newborn day.

The Seasons

Predictably and ever present
The seasons dance across the stage of life--
Soldiers of colour and hue;
Parade in conflagration to four- four measured step.
All decked out—uniformed uniformity,
Reward in medallions of rank and file
Marching through our days
As we stand and applaud.
Caught in penumbral shadow,
Half footed to our deeds,
Helpless to the passing of years to the last Shofar--
That Trumpet wherein we turn to face the final winter;
Definiens to the final Fall.

We Are No Longer Lovers

We are no longer lovers,
But, can we just pretend?
Perhaps to mend frayed tethers,
Before their weak threads rend.

Perhaps we could but savour
The straight before the bend—
Too late? Too late! We sever
The start before the end.

We are no longer lovers
Just awkward book-end friend,
Afraid to find the quire,
Where thoughts may well amend.

We are no longer lovers
But still a treasured friend?
Or have you found another
To have your heart attend?

Alas! To part, to wish-*"Fair Weather!"*
Where we should welcome home,
The love once bound together,
By Heaven's Golden Dome.

Tell me

Tell me-
Truly tell me!
When we kiss—
"What do you feel?"
What does this osculation seal?
A moment perhaps, of unfettered bliss?
Or just a duty in remiss.
What does this anatomical collision reveal?
--Two frozen lips as cold as steel?
--Two hearts that melt with ardent zeal?
Does desire, passion and fervour congeal?
To form a sweet and honeyed miel?

"Enough! Unbridled servility!
--Sufficient to fill a fawning fool's fob—
Such obsequiously craven sycophancy"

Tell me truthfully, honestly...
What do you feel as we rub lips in a kiss?
Ah! I thought so-
Nothing!
But a *bis*.

Forgive Me for Not Visiting

"Forgive me for not visiting you today!"
I thought of it; as I drove past the bay.
But, somehow I cannot bear the sight of you--
Too much to embrace, too vivid a view.

The road that leads to home was still there,
Straight and narrow as the shaft of a guiding spear.
I know that if I follow its path
It would lead me to your arms
Under the Flagler Palms.

It is too much to bear.
Today, I cannot spare another tear—
Seeing you under the shadow of the Oak
With the cold tomb stone as a cloak
Too solemn a sight too burdened a bier
I cannot bare another tear!

"Forgive me for not visiting you this day"
I remember too well when you went away.
On my next visit when my heart is colder then,
I will stop and sing to you under the garden glen.

You Are So Beautiful!

You are so beautiful!
Curly headed,
Eyes as chestnuts with a sparkle all their own;
Lips as red ripe cherries
And sweet as tender berries.

You are so beautiful!
Cradled in my arms I carried you across the world,
From snow and windy north
To hot and sunny south;

Your clutch like an angel's vise,
Secure and safe as the folds of rose petals.
Your infant fingers round as young snow apples,
Your voice so gentle; gentle as the wind through the Edelweiss.

"You are so beautiful,
So beautiful—
My son."

To Catherine

She wore a bright pink bonnet
With yellow flowers on it,
And dancing on a floret's face
A smile would skip and sit.

Dressed in a frilly frock of blue,
With circled waist band too,
Tied neat and snug with plaits of two
Hang bows in blended hue.

She tip-toed through a brothers' garden
All strewn with strange mischievous deed,
A battle field all boyhood trodden,
Could such a rosebud sow her seed?

But soon, so quick and brave she stood,
Unsure of deed embolden,
Yet took her place between the brood,
A stance that came too sudden!

Now seasons long with deeds all swollen
She holds the reigns of kin--
Her clan the Knox and Atkinson;
My dear sweet sister, Catherine.

Lines Written in Brazen Defiance of Old Age

Rise up!
Rise up!
You aged warrior;
Old bones may linger in the heel of age;
Yet sharp burns the spirit,
The muscled sting of astringent vinegar.

Rise up! Raise the curved but eager spine,
Unleash your might old man,
Don your vest of armour!
Take your sword of valour!
Let sing the scabbard's might and flavour.

There stands the upstart!
That old adversarial fool strutting his stride upon bright fields of green.
He counts death's souls as a money lender
Piling up the interest,
Cheating at the scales of justice;
Believing—fool that he is—that lines and fissures upon a weathered
cheek
Portends a crack in spirit;

"Stand firm!"
Plant your bones with youthful swagger!
He marches with strident vigour
Upon the Aged years left slender
By the relentless march of an unyielding time.

He will not break step with honour
Across these weakened bridges seasoned with the sweat of labour;
Nor lend compassion in deference to a venerable soldier.

Then turn you must!
You aged warrior. Turn!
Greet with countenance bold *Moira's* triplicity:

Spinner,
Allotter,
Unturnable--
Singing the songs to Sereines' yesterdays, today and tomorrows.

Turn you aged warrior turn!
Bristle with the tiger's bright burn
And with countenance stern
Turn your blade with might and zest—
Victory's drumming in an ageing breast;

Shake off the mounting years of wear and rust.
Stand fast! Quick thrust!
There! Leave such hoariness in the blood and dust.

I Drank a Little Too Much Wine

"I drank a little too much wine today"

I celebrate my
        Stay!
I feel the years fall deep and
        Hard

Upon this face of
        Clay.......

The Merlot
            Flows so deep and
        mellow
Toast to toast with
                        Chardonnay
Then turn to greet the
        Cabernet
And breathe its sweet
bouquet

        "I drank allot of wine today!"

"But what the
        hell!"
        "I do deserve it
        well"

"Now! Open up that Zinfandel!"

Snowfall:
Lines Written in Turbulent Perplexity

See! The snow falling to another dance in the yielding skies--
Flaked frenzy, cold ivory fireflies
Scattering;
This wintry umbrella shielding the summer's rays
Of retiring sunlight,
Waiting out her incubative days
Upon an eager ovum.
This repetitive repetition of seasoned seasons;
Tireless and unrelenting to the call of a demanding god.

"Does she not tire as I tire?"
Dispirited and flagging into a cavern of weary repose;
Even as I play the indigent patron
Gazing from the pit upon this theatre of encores--
Silently applauding the grim and inexorable scene.

I question:
"Bravery or cowardice?
Slavery or service?
Obedience or servitude?"
This fast and veracious marriage of the seasons,
Plighting and incorruptible to the troth of duty.

I turn to wander in once more upon this icy
Whip of a frozen charge;
Driving endlessly forward this chariot of turning wheels
Within wheels,
Ratcheting up a timeless conscious surrendering to its office;
And then to lope and canter in gloriously
To the triumphant and redemptive spring.

Why Did You not Come to Me My Love?

"Where are you my love?"
"You said you would come in the spring!".

I wait until the last flake of snow melts
Under the garden rosebush;

But you do not come!

The grey skies of winter are now melting,
And the timid sun untangles itself from the cold leash of winter-tide.

Carved upon this face of ice,
Under the shy moon's glow,
Looking upward to the star that will bring you home to me—
I stand to wait upon your vow.

But you do not come to me my love;
You do not come!

Now I fear the watchful glow of springtime,
The bloom of you in every flower.

Longing once more for the bleakness of winter
I hide from your presence,
Covering my ears from your laughter,
Shielding my eyes from the lurking light of a sentient spring.

Yet you do not come to me my love!
Still you do not come.

Welcoming; I turn to greet a gelid heel
Striding across my call--
Stilling my song,
Turning melody into mournful orison.

In abdication's claw forsaking all—
Under the shrouded skies where sombre stars
Disconsolate and woeful, weep upon this pyrrhic idyll—
I hug the cold bosom of loneliness,
Laying down my hope for your return.

"Look my love! Look!"
"Spring walks over my shadow;"
"Hidden within this biding burrow
Alone I lie; unrequited and forgotten!"

"Why did you not come to me my love!"
"Why did you not come?"

The Pubescent Dawn Rises

Fresh and with the scent of heather
The pubescent dawn rises!
Innocent and shy as a virgin maid----
She steps barefooted into the sun of awareness
Standing awkwardly innocent in the curved hip of white fleshed light;
Unsure and insecure she gives herself to me
As I peer into her melting shadows;
And I savour the lay
Round and running,
Hiding in the valleys of heather-scented sweetness
And rolling in her hills;
Drawing outward in praise of all that is beautiful.

I rise and take her in—
The dawn warm and giving;
Hyacinth upon heather we kiss
In marriage of blissful satisfaction,
Staining the union with the rich red blood
Of Spartan death and rebirth—
Heather incarnadine with Apollo's blessings,
The womanly dawn and I lay together
Until the rude fingers of a jealous noon disturbs our intimacy.

Age Wears a Gossamer Chain to Wisdom

Age oftentimes wears a gossamer chain to wisdom,
Shackled by the cunning shadows of perception.
Alas! Wisdom have I not worn well;
As for age?
It buries me deep within that hopeful act of rebirth—
An infant with a well worn thumb sucked dry by need.

Some call me Fool!
Perhaps foolish I am.
But the heart of an undeceitful fool bears neither malice nor cunning,
Just the awkwardness of a sometimes fawning buffoon—
Pleasing rather than unpleasing;
Obsequious for the sake of courting the cool winds of harmony.

Fool! Jester?
Which plays the comedic laughter,
Jocund and falling over in the act of frivolity?
But Clown? Never!
Painted into colours that fade with age
And glisten with the hypocrisy of circumstance—
Never true to the mask;
That two-faced doppelganger—
That demon in disguise.

Wisdom, Age,
Age, Wisdom—
Weathered experience that darkens the soul,
Perverting true intention.
Nay! Give me Agedom; pleats in the sheets of sweet slumber;
For I neither wear with honesty the night vests of true wisdom,
Nor with regret the sack cloth of age.

But Agedom? Yes, Agedom!
This have I worn well.
Striding out into a weathered world covered with chafed clouds
And effulgent sunshine,
Decked out in dark damp corners and bright getting-up mornings,
Bent over with burdened frame of weighty measures;
I laugh; not as the clown rehearsing an act of humdrum humour
Upon a worn out painted stage stained with yestreen's faceless paint;
Nor the jester, who tricks the King of Nonsense into the ways of the
pit full unwashed;
Neither as Fool—the wiser of the wings—who wisely laughs at himself--
But only through the roar of others.

But instead as Agedom—
That old grey owl that blinks and winks at the world,
Washing away with curtained-clothed eyes,
The useless repetitions of the ways of the blind.

Give me Agedom!
This I embrace and cuddle;
Nursing its welled-up experience with bosoms of honeyed sweetness;
For Agedom is but the better part of Wisdom—
Collimated through the curtains of time:
Diffracted by the resonance of experience,
Falling over the lip of eternity—without agendum—
Into timelessness that bears no suns,
Counts neither days nor years—
But embracing ubeity's presence in the illusive present,
In a manner as the waves ebb and flow into itself.

Ah! Agedom!
Blessed Agedom!
A Kingdom without end—
Eternal dominion immersed in the Kingdom of Light.

Looking Through My Window on a Snowy Day

Looking through my window on a snowy day-
Over the mountain of stones and window-caves clinging obtrusively
to the North sky,
I look down anxiously to the bare boned trees,
Quiet and asleep in peace and comfort,
Confident in the spring that cuddles in infancy.

A barren, bare, bold, sky sweeps clean its sleeping chimney,
Pouring down a dead lifeless ash upon a chilled bone earth--
Scattered snowflakes, free from heavens reposeful hearth
Sewing the changing sky together;
Flakes of frantic frozen fireflies fleeing an imprisoned heaven
Dancing before my own glass faced cell.

I sit motionless.
Observing the exodus to a promise of spring:
Each on its own course
Each on its own journey
Bound to its own mission
Driven by its own destiny--
Slavery's freedom dance to a hopeful rest;
All save one.
Just one compassionate heart that stops to greet me,
To pause and question my presence in its theatre of dance,
In its own time and season:

"Why look out with such sad eyes?"
"Why do you dream of a time long gone?"
"Why hold to hope that dies?"
"In the winter of now; in a time all done"

It lingers, it hovers in a prayer,
Still; amidst the fast moving traffic of its kin,
Too close to my window too close I fear,
Too close to the song that sang the sin.

I hear them calling him away to join their frolic and busy chatter,
I fear for his safety in my dark world,
And wish him fair flight and freedom's fortune
In his moist journey to the spring;
But alas! He drew too close to my salted view;
Trimming his wild free sails towards the rocks and shoals of my
window's glass
To bleed before my sight.
Such sacrifice!
Giving up his warm blood
Exchanging my cold tear
Leaving the promise of the salted sea to warm my saddened heart
On this cold and snowy winter's day.

As I look Upon Your Face

As I look upon your face; I see the rivers of senescence
Meandering;
Cutting with watery scalpel
The wild woeful panting of an enduring heart,
Lines and gorges running away deep within a channelled cheek
And there to bridge a buried smile upon a curl of lip.

But, to look into your eyes, therein I find the radiant youthfulness of
a summer's morn.
Perhaps your eyes portend no weight of time-
Neither recognition nor perception of change.

And to question;
Have your eyes filtered out with non-judgemental aperture
Through those dark green orbs,
The condition of all things being perfect in their current state?
Ubiety's song to wisdom?
Unconditional offerings of an impartial palm in praise of goodness,
Stirred by the apothecarist's hand into the brew of heart and mind
and soul.

The light I see has gathered up on journeys far
From worlds beyond measure,
All filtered through the prisms of the gods,
Arriving at the touch as pure untarnished gems—
Those silver patinas polished with the thoughts of Godness.

Is it then that Light that I drink from your eyes?
Have you sifted with tender compassion my imperfect vision?
That which dwells not in Milton's Holy Light but in the
Penumbral dissonance of Moira's deceptive edge?

Pray lend me your eyes to see the good in all,
Eyes that reflect only the pantings of a sacred vision,
Reverberations of the undefiled tiphereth;
Transform in me all base matter to Divinity's Light.

Now, as I look upon your face
I see beautiful tributaries running down deep into a grotto of sacredness;
Do I dare trace this dance along this sacred Pathway to the *centre.*
Will you share with me your Light that I may see more clearly
The Path that I have now forgotten?

To Francisco:
The Old Man Danced

He danced;
The Old Man—
Sifting through the rhythms of his youth
When he floated in young dreams and young hearts,
Touched by the charms of the Senoritas –
Dark eyed, dark haired, and skin so smooth.

He danced the old man the old man danced
Under the moon in the tropic light,
The old man danced and danced all night.

He danced,
The Old Man--
Turning in a circle, kicking up his heels,
Remembering the music of his tribe,
His arms in the night air, catching a moonbeam,
Cantillating in his heart the songs of his village folk.

He danced the old man the old man danced
Under the stars in the tropic night
The old man danced and danced all night.

He danced,
The Old Man—
Lifting his knees to the Castilian
An aged wrist in an elegant twist,
His swagger and dip, his turn now grander;
Losing the stoop of his years he stood taller.

He danced the old man the old man danced
Under the sky in heaven's sight
The old man danced deep into the night.

He danced!
The Old man—
Till the hills of his village rose with dawn,
And the roosters bugle that E Flat Horn,
In waltz with the dark woods of the *Caura* Valley
And the beckoning river on its way to the sea.

Still he danced!
The old man the old man danced--
Then he paused....
With a smile and a graceful bow
Old Man welcomed dawn's gladdening vow,
To slip away quietly home to keep,
So deep in the valley in the valley of sleep.

Who Is She?

Who is she who walks within her own space
Leaving behind not a trace
Of purpose or intent?
On her way to a land wherein she dwells
Alone
And unknown--
Ubiety's vagabond daughter in praise of elusiveness.
I watch her in the Fall's turning,
Leaning at a corner of a leaf covered street,
Her bright coloured scarf an antithetical presence
To her evanescent shadow,
Flapping like a sail in the hint of winter's wind---
Her phantom figure smeared across a dying autumn's lay.
I try to read her thoughts from far away,
Transient as they may,
Sending warm wishes running through the chill of day:

"Be well strange woman!"
"All wrapped up in woolen thoughts"
"Please taste my wish"--
Though strange, though distantly disconnected.

Under the street lamp
She turns; as if to welcome my deep questioning;
But embracing legerity's nimbleness she falls away from sight.

This strange woman leaves not a trace;
Not a stain upon the canvas of space,
But in my distant world she leaves her grace—
A solitary soul without a face.

Eccentricoleman

Eccentric old man:
Wild in his ways,
Unconventional—
Relic.

He questions even the sun in its orbit.
Away from the centre,
An axis to himself—
Eccentric Old Man rotates in his own universe.
Contrary and oppositional, this primordial soon-to-be-cadaver
Views the sky not as a blanket of blue infinity,
But rather a personal park-bench-
His rusted resting place for his hoary hindmost to hover;
And to stare upon a heaven; complaisant in jock-itched thoughts
That there is no place else to go but up!
Naked---except for his beard,
He wraps his rusted self with moonbeams
And views the craters in that golden orb as reflections of his non-venerable face.

EOM dines in his own time,
Breaking the day with fare victuals;

"To hell with expectedness!"
"I eat only what I care for".

Wine replaces coffee at dawn;
--Roots and nuts at lunch—
This fossilised fragment finds favour in the music of the running stream.
He entertains himself in counting falling autumn leaves—
An intricate abacus of colour and shape,
Conceptualised and perceptualised by EOM's own law;
Each falling leaf a deed that he had done and done well in his own way;
Leaves that remain will all but await his moth-eaten transmutation.
Contented in content and contentment---He then farts for self-applause—
Pre-prandial and postprandial—aperitif and digestif—
Self-servings to a well appointed table.

This Palaeolithic fragment of primordial yesterdays bathes between the raindrops--
He never washes--
Such would suggest uncleanliness,

"Odour is kind to the otherwise orphaned senses"

But to bathe with the raindrops is a baptism of thanks
For heavens sacramental tears.
This old tatterdemalion rag pays homage to the raindrops bubbles--
Bowing over in wonderment at their purposeful intent
Disappearing down the jaws of earth's porous appetite;
Deep down in the depths of ancient roads that he has travelled
Leaving musical murmurs of past songs that he has sung
Deep beneath the surface of his world.

Lines Written in Despair and Despondency

To My Island Home.

Vised between the Black and Brown,
The pale emerges sickly and anaemic.
Starved and weak—voiceless in the call
To Erob's long faded sun
Where Zeus wooed Europa to lie upon her bosom.

Set and bled upon a history parched with warfare and the conqueror's sword;
Sexton and gilded trade give way to the black smoke of a new time and voice
And those now left behind—deformed and lost upon a lonely landscape.
Such lays this corpse, bloodless and pale,
Stretched out and vulnerable,
Unattended between the valleys' closing jaws;
Lowered by time and travel of history's weighty boot.
Contented in malcontent, embracing fear and trepidation,
Resignation's boot upon the neck of timidity's dishonour.

Land of my father!
Bosom of my mother!
Such evil have we wrought upon the stones that lay upon a timeless
native shore—
Now brought to bear unmercifully in Milton's prophetic law.
This fruit of paradise lost and gone forevermore;
Given up by neglect and greed
This promise a promise no more,
This green emerald,
This sardine gem to precious freedoms.

O Eire! Caribbean green-
Your Native song sung amongst the sister hills that kiss a starry heaven.
O Conquerabia! Land of old dreams and hopefulness
Your waves now stain our shores with crimson blood.
O Port-of-Spain! Your Dragon's Mouth that fed a world afar
And wooed the courtly princess's hand.
O Trinity! Ruler of all heavens we kneel in contrite remorse.

Now vised between the Black and Brown,
The Pale, hostage unto itself awaits its own demise;
Offering a shackled neck,
Pale and milky in the austere sun,
Awaiting the flash of silver blade of steel;
Listening for the timid bleat—
Of disembodied head upon Prince Frederick's dusty street.

Valediction

A silent room
A withered flower
A tear drop's tomb
A dying ember
Darling!
I clothe my sadness in the darkness you leave behind
Your kiss sentient and lingering—
Sweet orchids to the evening's hush
Tears and tears
Silver milk bleeding upon a doleful cheek
Torrential offerings to a turning heart
A closing door
Striking a bellowing gong forevermore.
A moaning breeze, sympathetic and healing
Ardour
Fervour
Love's need no more.

If Dreams Be the True Side of Life

If dreams be a true side of life,
Then let me dream and never wake;
For it is here that I am home.
Such vagaries in which to play,
Such reveries to light a darkened way;
There are no limits in my dream--
I run on wings,
The dark night sings,
Colours never fade,
Even in the Oak and shade
The sun can wade between the rings
Of age and silent mossy glade.

In my dream all is fragrant,
In my dream all seem green and radiant.
This visitant haunt of light and truth
Dispels the myth grotesque;
No chimera dare disturb the songs of reverie
Where lives and sights and premonitions harmoniously
Strum the angels' melody.

In my dream she never frowns;
In my dream she is always young
And finds me with her thoughts.
I am never lost; in my dream—
Even in strange places
There are familiar faces
That I once loved; both with heart
And in reverential due;
There to sit upon a comforting knee;
And then to hold within a youthful palm
A cheek and lock and chin and lip of balm.

If dreams are where I find sweet memory,
If dreams are where I sing truth's melody
That fades within my awakened scenes;
Then let me dream--
From dream to dream to dreams.

Though yestreen's shade be shy in coming—
Let me dream.

Love Is Not Born!

Love is not born until we rub eyes in gentle agreement.
Smiles pucker in a rosebud's stance
And opens its petals with a nod.
Approving a wordless call—
I follow;
You lead.
Under the moon's embrace—
A kiss!
Singing with a heaving heart
A bosom's aver cry of want;
And with legerity's dance
I oblige upon the quick of tenderness.
What sounds of resignation disturbs the night bird's sleep--
Restful and resting under the wing of slumber's coil;
Voyeurs to a dance thrown wide and flung open
In cantillation to a syzygistic sky in royal approval
Of our communion of hearts.

Such is sentience song to this stillness of time,
In absentia to all but us,
To weld together
In fusion by love's purposeful embrace,
Amain in praise of joyful acquiescence.

Love is not born until we smoke
By alchemy's hand in noble stoke
And then to lie in cinders deep
Two hearts of ash in a smouldered heap.

O Heaven!

O Heaven!
Laid out in carpet blue;
Curling over my sight far out upon the seat
That sits the ever dancing stars.

O Heaven!
Canopy of wonder,
We tremble at your vastness.
Where do you begin?
How far do you run?
Sailing past the baubles we name the stars,
Littering your endless chase
Into the lap of space.

O Heaven!
Childhood wonder,
Wherein we glimpse the Angels standing at the corners,
Smoothing out the blue linen
Slept upon by passing saints on triumphant ride to Glory.

O Heaven!
Ageless Madonna,
Fertile womb of wonder,
Eden's hips to perpetual maternity
Embracing us your terrified progeny.

O Heaven!
Falling in an orb,
Over the seas that seals your slit of lips;
Heaven and earth with my silent kiss.
Goodnight!

If You Love me

Discourse with Dubiety

"If you love me
Then say that you do,
What are you afraid of?
That perhaps I do too?"

Why hide in the veil of pretension?
If you love me,
There should be no hesitation.

"Just say it!"
Three small words
Thus; *"I love you!"*

Three small words that makes a whole new world—
Though frightening and fraught with dubiety's fulfilling.

"Why so afraid to love?"

--Perhaps because with it comes loss?
Such loss!
So complete!
Loss of one's self...
Set adrift in a tide of unknowing—
A freefall into an unknown forest
Abundant with exotic trees that bear strange fruit and flower
That we fear to pluck and savour
And taste their flavour.

"Ah..."

"If you love me?
Then tell me you do--
There is nothing to fear,
For I too,
Do!"

Immolation:
Lines in Honour of the Christian Martyrs of the Near East

Cry! The gory wave bears full ignominy--
The sap of bones and blood made sacred by sacrifice pure;
Courage! Bold and brazen sings amidst the sands of stark savagery.
We stand upon the City Hill bathed white in Light;
And there in Prayer; we stare
Upon a helpless sheep,
Corralled to the furnace flames.
The rising shadow curved in Crescent curl
Strike! Scymetre's slice severed to a scarlet seam--
That merciless brush within the painter's hand;
With daggers intent,
Slicing the sacred canvas with a crimson slit.

Sweet Sacrifice! Sacred Hymn to souls that serve;
Silently bowing into the valley of supplication.

But we, who bear the Cross of freedom's rage
Born upon that said Hill;
Where Crown of Thorns won with blood upon Redemption's cry—
Stand once more;
Not upon the knee of Worship's gaze,
Nor strike a breast through orison's tearful haze,
Instead to shout to Heaven's Portals, "Praise!"

"Rise up ye soldiers of the Cross!

"We sing your scrolls of triumphant unfolding"

"O Unvanquished Souls!"

"Nailed and riveted to the Cross of Sacrifice"

"We cry God for freedom"

"God for victory"

"De profundis!"

"Ad majorem Dei gloriam!"—"To the great glory of our God".

A Sign of the Unkindness of Becoming a Man

A sign of the unkindness of becoming a man;
To leave behind in the wake of childhood
A misty memory of a carefree dance;
Where the music never ceases:
Those rising rhythms, riotous and raw--
Sensual, seductive and sentient,
All in swaddle to delicious dissonance;
That symphonic cacophony in deference to the wide eyed awakenings
of self;
A sudden vivication from the dream world--
Rousing and restless; from the rout of juvenescence
To the sadness of the Knowing.

To leave behind an unquenched tastefulness—
Wanton, wayward in vagabond's dressage
To an unbridled canter;
Young Man! Serpentine and impulsive;
Stay on the bit!
Collect your paces for the jump;
Transition to impending fences of a merciless course,
Where the boyhood dance gives way to flight,
Where only security's approach can nail your hooves upon an
Inexorable fate.

Young man! Green to the sap of sin;
Armed you are, sure footed in your swagger,
Schooled from a frothy youth--
Prepare!
Button up; armour to the chin—
Let conquest be your praise.

Seas and earth and sky are all but gifts to a valiant heart.
Our eyes will not meet again, Young Man;
Yet, our hearts will remember;
Ripe and red and resplendent, those days we spent together;
Fair well, Fare well; and Farewell!

Lover, Send Me Kisses

Lover!
Send me kisses for which I do not ask,
For asking dulls the treasured task
Tainted by a journey fraught by my need;
And void of your readiness free and giving
From a heart full and brimming.

Lover!
Send me kisses freely,
For if I ask, then comes a loss, made weighty by an iron will
And not a gentle heart.

Lover!
Send me kisses which I do not seek,
But kisses that finds within its pith
Its own desire to free itself from thee;
Made ready as an eager bee
To mount a sacred flower,
Moist and giving of its flowing nectar.

Lover!
Do not fill my need—but yours.
Send me kisses that heals an abscess
Heart; weighty with the milk of your tenderness.

Lover!
Allowance to suckle; ripe and voracious,
Succour to wring from me all claim
And then to sleep with breathless orison—
Tender to the very pore,
Upon satiety's blustery repose,
Weighty, helpless and contented.

Lover!
Gorge thyself!
Drink and thirst no more--
Ambrosia offerings to a clamouring heart,
Requisite and resigned to your appetence.

Lover!
Desideratum complevit.

Glove:
In Praise of Giving a Glove at Banff, Alberta

Hail! To warm a winter's chill
And turn the sting of ice into a cresting wave of warmth
Finds such simplicity;
This gesture's kindness--
Ample and overflowing.
But, since ineptitude of mortal acts-
Entrenched in its own being
Espy paucity,
Harness then, sweet labour's effulgence—
Generosity's milky sustenance;
And let what is left in dearth of giving
Find full measure,
And treasure,
In gratefulness.

To L.: Basso Cantante

We once rubbed the raw red earth between our lives
And stumbled on;
Broken at times:
Afflicted and disillusioned,
Betrayed;
Defamed;
Woeful and wronged—
Dishonour heaped upon a generous spirit;
Where symmetry's scheme, laid out with steadfast propriety
Unto the affirmed law of patrimonial fidelity.
Such devotion! Sanctified upon committal altars
Only to fall upon the serrated edge of disloyalty.

Still, but never silent,
Together, we sang sonorously;
Songs in tempii true,
Melody's woven web a dance within our hearts.

This man we knew; his song we envied with the sweetness of true deference:
Now, a song no more.
Refrain in hush.
Risibility's canter no longer.
Yet, that smile that tore the sunset's veins
In fissures of true blooded radiance,
Still sails across an evening's sky.

Hail Cossack!
Laid out in princely cassock,
Triumphant at the Celestial Danube—
Till then, till then!
When the light of new and welcomed day
Joins our palms once more in the flesh of friendship's clasp;
We will remember you in the deep bass rhythmic beatings of our hearts.
Proschaij!

To Charlie: On His Birth

Your gift of loins run deep and sound
Upon God's fertile land,
Such blessed seed will long abound--
Your Valdez Arms will stand.

True blue upon its trusted dreams--
From far Asturias
Silver's hue! A crest now gleams--
"To Charlie's birth!"-America's.

In praise of Peter's Waldensians stance
Of centuries long ago,
Alaska's seal; his naval lance—
Admiral; Knight, Antonio.

Perhaps when scrolls and seals are smitten—
Upon the misty swirl of time;
Some will ask and much be written—
Songs of our Father's name in rhyme.

Perhaps young Charlie asks one day,
In the spring of a flowered May—
"Who is this Frank?" "Whose bones now lay?"
In the warmth of the Palm Coast Bay.

Song To You

Please let me sing to you
With longing breath I cling to you,
Though tears have left a furrowed stain
Let me sing again!

Please let me sing once more
With all my heart I do implore,
I stand upon an empty shore
To glimpse your eyes once more.

"When I walk through a meadow my thoughts are of you
With ev'ry step I make
When I see a rolling cloud I think of you
And joyful breath I take"

I beg to sing to you
On wings of song it rings so true,
Through sleet and snow and icy rain
Let me sing again!

My Love, to sing to you
With aching heart I bring to view,
Those memories of years gone by
When we were young and shy.

"Your name on morning's breath I hear
The dew in sorrow's tear
From lips as rose bud sweet and red—
A tender scented bed"

Please let me sing to you
My pleading heart I fling you,
I wait beside an open door
To hear your voice once more.

My Love! My songs still soar
With fading kiss, a *"je t'adore,*
Now you have crossed through heaven's door
Alas! I sing no more!

With Kind Eyes

I have grown much older since;
Perhaps you may—with eyes as kind swab—
Mop away the imprints of a well travelled man,
Seasoned with the sauces of sentience,
Sorrowful and gloriously chastised
With the whips and chains of wisdom's code.
This vagabond's journey through acuity's throb and quick,
Laid out upon memory's membrane
All the soreness; pica to the appetite of a well seasoned soul.

Still and in stillness,
Unmovable to all but you—
My heart remains a tender crucible;
Wherein with willingness—stirred with apothecary's bowl and spoon,
Mixed with gentleness and purpose pure--
The taste and lasting memory of moments monumental—
All well kneaded into the sweetness that is the kindness in your eyes.

O God! Your Winter Comes

O God! Your winter comes—a slap upon a summer's cheek;
With stern severity in reprimand to the servile service of true hearts---
Gratitude in praise of full measured mercy and forgiving scrolls of
promised salvation—
I sleep in one tender constant:
Immovable,
Cemented,
Tenderly buried above her smile--
Sunlit and warm,
Riveted in bolts of plight and troth,
Nailed in with fervent hammers,
Strapped tight and cured with leather bound,
Chained with links of iron,
Measured and treasured with patient sacrifice—
Such a love; averred in upon Heaven's Paradise.

Your winter, O God,
Comes buried in her eyes and under the curl of her lips;
A dungeon sweet and stark—
Cold in bone upon a kneeling stone,
There, crouched up in a bundle,
Possessing all and giving freely
Fair rests my warm heart; meekly
Sentenced to the jailer's throne.

Oh God! Set free, let ride
Upon the lonely gallows; guide
Garrotted to fidelity's crown—
Let Fall!
Turning in quiet sacrifice, to the East—
Tangled, taught and tightly bound;
A broken fruit upon an unforgiving stem,
Picked to pieces by the Merciful Dove.

O God! Your winter comes—
Cold sacrifice-
Glorious Redemption!

The Painter:
Lines in Praise of My Brother

The poised and regal rose
And sweet stained fragrance of the flower,
Brought to life from the white nothingness
Of a dead canvas-- opaque and anemic,
Is such honoured prize.

To give life to a barren sky woefully wailing
For a single star to fill her vapid void
Is yours to favour and savour;
And make to hang
Upon the walls of dull and empty hearts--
Such is your true labour.

To colour thought with line and rhythm,
To slice nicely the seams of secret scenes
All wrapped up in a past long devoured by seasons feast—
Eternising nature's romp and roving rage--
Those jaws herbivorous, green in tongue and teeth,
Romping through fields of coloured readied reds,
Captured by your hand,
Is but your worth.

Such wonder in your world of coloured thoughts,
Images brushed to life by your heart's will,
And we, all penurious and wanting,
Dearthful in this deed of artful style;
May sit and dream and find ourselves in these images--
Tactile and rolitant.
By your hand, by your deed, by your volition to a lifeless brush
Swift and skilfully drawn from a darkened sky,
The wide and opened birth of a lifeless eye.

To take from nature its secret soul and set it down
For all to see—with your eyes,
Is averred the art of a new vision's birth,
For none can see with your eyes
Nor stroke with your sentience
Nor seduce upon an open canvas
The myriad charms of natures beckoning;
Herein lies your dance—your patina pentimento.

Rest

Stay in the saddle
Though the nag is old
Hang-on to the reins
Pray the stirrups hold
Over the mountains and into the west
Across the wide plains to the homestead's rest;

The light in the window
Makes the heart gather hope
Now, into the burrow
On a threaded rope;

No more! Cold nights
Nor hot desert days;
Save the cool calm wind across sunny bays;

Gone are the tears
Gone are the fears
Death to sorrow
Death to woe
No more to weep
No harvest to reap...

O sweet slumber! Reposeful and deep;
Welcome old rover to the soil of sleep.

Regret

The flower that fails to blossom,
The fruit that withers on the stem,
The stream that bundles-up stinking in its waste--
Moribund and thick with scum upon the dead branch
Lying in rude squat,
Across the purposeful duty of the stream's simple song
On its dream to the sea.

Herein lay the feast and fatness and fecundity of nature's bountiful
fields of regret—
Valleys, streams and rivers---a trough in which to drown her travail.

Should she lean against the weight of circumstance?
Or resign herself self into an eddy—
Endlessly turning in its time,
Quarrelling with the rocks,
Squabbling over the moss that was its own making.

To welcome the sleep of regret when tenacity's tide finds full flow
Is but to be in fool's favour;
For pensive thought in the bone of sweat opposes the sinews and
muscles of force and action.

To watch an oak leaf fall in absence of a tear
Is apathy's sinful neglect---
Knowing in the wisdom of self that the green sap soon must succumb
To the sanguine and orange pus that stifles the green dye—
That foison sweetness to a summer's day.
But, to drown in regret for the summer's glow
Is to curse the winter's snow;
Knowing full well that with its thaw,
Brings full vats to a well drunk spring,
Playful and giddy and drunk with laughter's colour.

Where weaves wisdom's worth?
To pause? To think? To ponder in ennui's lap?
--Only to bemoan a murky past, that perhaps,
Had fortune borne a benevolent bestowal bonnet
It may have chanced some exotic outcome;
Altering its state to suit some friendly fashion.

Shall the heart be then changed to comforting lament?
And wash its self-inflicted bruises with yesterday's tears;
Finding false solace in fervent wishes and dreams
To savour and kiss and drool over in mounds of tasteful regret?

Regret! Remorse!
Such wasting in the season of now;
In search of self proprioception is the path of the penitent
To espy the true Light
Between the wild thicket's growth
And there; in full bloom-- sits salvation.

Here, now! It's time to change the river's course
And sweep away the stench of decay and bones of yesteryears;
And guide the simple stream singing on its way to the sea.

Alas! To look back in Lot's fashion;
Oh! Sweet tears!
Tender in the pith of infant's embrace,
A sad but satisfying bouquet of regretful roses,
Ripe with teat of full bosom's milky regret;

Oh! Rueful Sorrow, steeped in misty grief--
Such delicious doleful pain,
Pressing upon that sweet tender nerve—
Soft chains of a regretful time made to simmer in tearful rust.

Such is Regret!

Do Not Stare

Do not stare!
For here lies the mossy run of years:
Elderly ivory—
Stained to the root,
Chewed out and all yellowed up.

Rather, with kind arms cover
And leave unattended by eyes youthful and tender
The furrowed trails of a wayfarer:
Battle armour bruised,
Bayoneted,
Rivets pulled,
Seamed and severed,
Seared and scorched,
Peripatetic and vagrant,
Stumbling over the cobblestones of discipleship,
In pale mimesis
To Orpheus' sacrificial ride to faithfulness.

But if you must:
View in half light—deceitful dusk;
Those convenient tardy shadows of cloaked concealment—
--Chiara Oscura---
Penumbral dissonance
To a phantom portrait of lambent, foamy youth.

Cover your eyes from shame;
Cloak with brisk compassionate glances;
Oh! Be a gentle voyeur and paint in dusky shades,
Furtive strokes upon this opaque canvas;
Chain those sanguine remnants of a fleeing sun
Holding fast discarded droppings of watery colours--
That past splendour of puerile yesterdays
Past and splendid no more---
Drooling now, upon the chin of a slack and aged sunlight.

Pray, hide within kind memory—
Where once, all stood straight--
Confident within your bended bow.
Place with kindness fair guillotine
And accept a tithing gesture for such act of forgiveness,
Before the sharp light of your eyes catch the falling blade,
Revealing ignominy's nakedness.

Now, last irrevocable look back over the pursuing legs of a merciless time—
Driving ample amain to the Muses' song
To that valley,
Set between heathered hills,
And there to lie without opprobrium,
Resignation unrevoked and undetected by the prying eyes of ridicule;
Let slide upon acquiescence silken surrender,
Challenged by freedom's assent—
Behold! The seam of mystery;
Unencumbered by frail and fragile hoary age—
--For it matters not how much the shine—
Offerings instead to the brass brazen bone buried between bare beauty.

Now nested;
Unleash the shackled fires of freedom's youthful dance,
Here, here! In the cloak of this moonlit forest—
I sing for you a song upon the lyre's breast of time that none has ever
sung before.

Saint Valentine's Day

On this winter's limb I kneel,
Transfixed by the weight of a gelid heel,
This stretching graveyard-- an entombing vise,
Encasing all in her breath of ice.

The birds all flown to a summer's land,
Leaving all covered by a white shadow's hand:
And I long for a kiss
For a moment of bliss
And the warmth of hips
Just the brush of lips.

The rose bush holds its flower--
Entwined as a lover,
Rolling in the music of their scented aroma;
Arboreal souls, in sweet moments of labour
They kiss; whisper endearments and flood
With caresses their petals of blood.

Yet I hold nothing but an indigent heart,
Wandering amongst the stars; apart
From tenderness, seeking out a lost and vagrant embrace,
Lost in the chaos of time and space:
Longing for the sweetness,
Seeking out the bliss,
Searching for the promise
Buried in that kiss.

Where Are You, Dear?

Where are you Dear?
Are you still there?
--Just a warm thought to burn a winter's ear—
All snuggled in tight?
Wrapped in winter layers?
--Sleep deep and rolling in your dreams—
Perhaps the impudent beams
Of a lost and wandering spring
May find an early song to sing;
Precocious though, she may leak
Her gentle kiss upon a flaxen cheek,
Worn pale and silken
By the soft fingertips of snowflakes; driven
From a grey secluded heaven.
Sleep!

Though starved of your presence,
Imprisoned by time's unmerciful sentence;
Be still!
I sprinkle you with starlight;
Shovelled in by endearing thoughts upon your counterpane of flaccid
repose;
I see you bundled in coiled-up comfort,
Asleep in peaceful abandon.
Sleep!

Flung wide,
Thrown deep,
Careless,
Fretless
Thoughtless—
Loose and slack in sinking slumber,
Unperturbed and unafraid,
No imp shall storm these gates secure
Nor will sacrilegious thoughts endure
Upon this scene pellucid pure.

Sleep deep!
Standing guard am I;
Wide eyed vigilance in sentinel stance,
Crossed with *Michaelian* Garbed Lance.

Does Love Grow Old

Does love grow old?
--Gather moss and mould--
Does the heart tire
Or lose its nascent fire?
Does the open palm
Still offer its sacred balm?
Does the eye find durst?
Does the ear still thirst?
When at first
The soughs--sweet sighs cause the heart to burst?

Does love grow old and tire?
Does the heart lose its desire?
Is the giving now for hire?
Are the song and the singer and the marriage to the lyre
All written, all scored, all sung by the choir?

What is then left for the heart to sire?
But the quire to the fire;
--To lie to rest on this sacred pyre.

River Bed:
A Hymn to Him

To look back at the once surging river
Now all dry with bones of stone;
And trace with watery eyes--familial fingers,
Along the curves and bends and miniature bays
And tender sways of solace and untroubled days.
From beck and burn and rill to runnel run,
And roam and rove upon meanderings sightless curves;
And pause to watch a quick and daring gallop to the ponds of calm
and silent treasure;
There to listen to the sweet song it sang on its way to the salient sea
In warm welcome to a tireless journey.

That gentle cool spray--
Silver and grey,
Turning a steady head into a heady wind
With quiet murmur and ripple
And open smile and cheerful chuckle.

Now still; the roving river
Dry and dead upon a pleading branch;
Pooling up upon an oxter's clutch, leafy and ripe with the sap of a
soulful spring--
Intent to savour and secure the last cool drink of this sweet stream,
Before the sap of salt dissolves its song into the wide waves of a
wayward sea.

To walk upon this barren bed,
Bereaved and broken but ripe with robust tribute,
And trace this orphaned course now left to mourn a rolling runnel's run;
And place a kindred palm onto this face of memory
And there, to trace upon this worn out face--
Rolling tears of fondness; in reminiscence to its mighty past—
This river bed strewn with all its daring deeds.

Now, to walk upon these dreams all dreamt
And stop to ponder;
And bend in honour to lift the buried stones
And unearth the treasure--
Monuments to a course all run.
And there, still there in faithful sacrifice—
Behold! Mnemonic to our tearful eyes,
A heart still lies
All damp and moist with tears so tender--
This barren bed, this silent river
Left behind in full passim
To his joyful Hymn.

Loss: To Imogene

Here lay our bold affairs
That which we savour
Through tide of anguish and of fears;
And to espy with tender tears
The cargo lost to discord and malcontent.
But to rest with contentment—
All who tried but yet in vain
To stem the tide and ride the flood,
And then to rest and let the current pull
Where lay its closed intent.

We can no more—mates of the *Imogene Maiden*—
Look back towards her cry that cut so clear
The neat night air—
Warding off the pending storm
And warning of the rocks that lie ahead.
Her lighthouse dim and dull and in the distance lie--
Lost in the rising fog of time.

We have with sextant true, failed to chart a course
That in good time would drag our oars upon a sandy bottom--
Anchored sure in restful repose;
Instead, we still the lonely bell upon the lighthouse lost—
A dimming Parola helpless in deed,
Screaming to the North Star in marriage annulled,
To the beckoning harbour of solace.

Again, Mates—all sea burnt bare and blistered with the sting of salt
We turn about;
We catch the wind,
We feel the lash;
Hearts lain out upon a barnacled hull—
Torn and opened to a scurvy sore
We rise to slap the impudent waves,
Again to sail once more to that ever ebbing shore.

Perhaps upon a cresting wave shackled to a hope filled horizon--
With sails trimmed and purposed full in binding intent,
We may, high upon the poop of hope
Lay our sea-burnt eyes upon a lip of land;
And wait for the joyful green leaf of promise,
Sent upon a sympathetic tide,
To quicken the heavy heart of despair
And place to shouts of joy,
Our voice upon a faithful wind.

Until then mates, scabbed by the blacksmith's sun,
To an open sea bound to a white and sandy shore,
We muster full passage once more,
To those green hills that lie between the ocean's door.

Indeed, if such be our choice
To chart a last course and log its days to this end voyage
Of our crew;
Here then we trim our sails no more—
Our gallant ship we set to wreck itself upon a rocky shore.

All Done

All done.
Next year to join the aged.
Bundled up in time's cocoon.
Wrapped securely with worn out bedding
To keep the bones from falling out.

To look back over a past that bends away--
Swallowed within the mist of this hazy day
Is but to shudder and roll in the chains of an unfettered past.

It matters not what then was done.
For all is flushed away as on a rainy day.
Sweet running tears all mopped up.
Memories, drowned in a bottomless cup.

Wiped clean ephemeral smiles and unto vaults
Secured and stamped with eternity's assaults.

Now paled the sanguine cheek once warm and bloodied bold
Faced heaven's east in genuflection to a rising day;
Interned by the blinding storms of winter's night
A face beneath; buried bland and tight.

Where rests risibility's ring?
Cachinnation clarion call in glad gusto to glorious youth—
Once reaching out upon an open street
Embracing all that it would meet--
Gone!

Such was the raging storm of youthful invincibility.
Sitting now, before the darkened door
Made dark by sinful lore--
This shadowy form
With hands all wrinkled worn,
Reposed upon a useless lap
Suctioned dry of phloem flowing sap.

Oh! Inactive uselessness,
Awaiting the coming dust storm,
Uprooted now the last stubborn shrub from the tongue of thoughts.
Scrubbed pale from this gray face of clay
With nothing left to say.

When all the tasks lay piled up high
Upon satisfactions last relieving sigh.
All bundled in:-
Rolled up
Under-taken
Done.

APERTURE

Richard Claude Valdez

Trafford Publishing www.trafford.com
Copyright 2009 Richard Claude Valdez

Aperture is a collection of poems drawn from life's experiences
and reflected through the emotional lens of love, joy, pain,
disappointment, anguish, loneliness and exhilaration.
It is an opening by which the 'light' of simple
human experience is collimated or diffracted.
Subjective though it may be, the poet sacrifices his mood,
temperament, disposition and personality at the altar of
expression. Aperture affirms that this emotion is the great
leveler, and that mankind—the embodiment of pure
emotion—drowns in the depths of its gentle wrath.

Promise of the Rainbow through My Tears

Richard Claude Valdez

Trafford Publishing www.trafford.com
Copyright 2001 Richard Claude Valdez

Promise of the Rainbow Through My Tears is a collection of romantic, lyrical and metaphysical poems, together with songs and ballads. The themes are a roving vagabond's stroll amongst images, scenes and telling experiences. Some reflect profound memories—pleasant and unpleasant—seen through the eyes of childhood and adolescence. Some are filled with a young man's romance and filled with rhyme and imagery. While others are introspective and searching—an old man's coming to grips with his mortality.

Above all, these poems tell the story of life's journey; from the cradle, along the dream of life, and to the grave and beyond.

The poems themselves are not divided into any particular order or theme; they roam much like the author's experiences and gather their own rhythm as their theme dictates. Although the poetic style of rhyme is not popular in modern poetry, much can be found throughout this collection, which accents the author's nonconventional approach to his work.

What is evident though are the varied themes reflected in this volume, which suggests that any reader will find some poem or line that would draw on his or her personal experience.

AUTHOR BIOGRAPHY

Richard Claude Valdez was born in Port-of-Spain, Trinidad. He attended Our Lady of Fatima College, under the tutourship of the society of Holy Ghost Father—founded in 1703 at Paris.
Richard left Trinidad for studies in Canada at the University of Toronto and the Royal Conservatory of Music; he resides in Toronto.

A classical vocalist in the field of Opera and Concert, Richard has performed throughout the world. He was recently awarded significant recognition for his contribution to the cultural life of Canada—Trinidad & Tobago in Canada, 1962—2012.

East of Goodbye is his third volume of poetry; his other volumes are Aperture, published in 2009, and Promise of The Rainbow through My Tears, published 2011.

Together with his international performances and his writing, he has added musical composition to many of his poems which he performs at the concert platform.

Adding to his vagabond career as teacher, civil servant, manual labourer, business entrepreneur to name just a few--bounded by the United States; London, England; Germany; Tobago and the tiny islands of Monos and Gasparee off the coast of Port-of-Spain, Trinidad-- Richard still finds the time to Sky Dive from 13,500 feet over his adopted homeland of southern Ontario, Canada.

ALPHABETICAL LIST OF FIRST LINES

A sign of the unkindness of becoming a man
A silent room
Age oftentimes wears a gossamer chain to wisdom
All done
Alone to grieve
Amidst the triangular blue spruce
And what say the moon
And where is she?
As I look upon your face, I see the rivers of senescence
Cry! The gory wave bears full ignominy
Do not stare!
Does love grow old?
Eccentric old man
Empty now to stand empty
Feathered butterfly sailing pass
Flame nailed to a tree
Forgive me for not visiting you today
Fresh and with the scent of heather
Hail! To warm a winter's chill
He danced
Here lie our bold affairs
I cannot bear to harvest
I drank a little too much wine today
I have grown much older since
If dreams be a true side of life
If this be earth!
If you love me
It is too much!

Know now that all must have its time
Leaves fall and are dissolved away by time
Looking through my window on a snowy day
Love was not born before we rubbed eyes in gentle agreement
Lover!
Now we speak in riddles
O Heaven!
O Time!
O! To be like tulips
Oh God! Your winter comes—a slap upon a summer's cheek
On this winter's limb I kneel
Please let me sing to you
Predictably and ever present
Rise up!
See! The snow falling to another dance in the yielding skies
She wore a bright pink bonnet
Sombre shades of Autumn drapes its shadowy arms
Stay in the saddle
Still the Neanderthal
Streets are quiet
Talmid
Tell me, truly tell me
The flower that fails to blossom
The morning breaks like the slow quiet dribble of a new born infant
The poised and regal rose
There is a great loss here
This and more is but the love so shared and given
To look back at the once surging river
To sleep on many a stranger's kindness
Today shapes the bones of a fall day
Under the eerie mist of time
Vignette
Vised between the black and brown
Walk with me by the water
We are no longer lovers

We once rubbed the raw red earth between our lives
What is this tear
When the fresh salted tears of a sad parting
"Where are you Dear?"
"Where are you my love?"
Which sword first sliced the salted waters of my island home?
Who is she who walks within her own space
"Woman! Woman?"
You are so beautiful
Your call today settles my heart into a gentle throb
Your gift of loins run deep and sound

Printed in the United States
By Bookmasters